Addictions

Our Use of Chemicals, Denials and Other Distractions

Loran Joly

Contents

Chapter One

We are all Addicts, it looks like!

First of all, the author maintains that all of us are addicts, each in our way.

For we all use Defense Mechanisms, as Freud talked of.

Call these Habituated Defense Mechanisms of Choice, or Drugs of Choice, or Crutches, or what have you.

Only, instead of having Chosen these, the author would suggest that These have CHOSEN US.

And so, hence, this video to support that idea:

Why We Are All Addicts

https://youtu.be/f55QO2isoKM?si=gJKKx1GNvyFJO4JB

Or, too, as Dr. Anne Wilson Schaef has related, in:

https://a.co/d/aNgCs4g

When Society Becomes an Addict Paperback

https://a.co/d/a2MI2zS

Anne Wilson Schaef (March 22, 1934 – January 19, 2020) was an American clinical psychologist and author. Her book *When Society Becomes an Addict*, in which *she compared Western culture to an active alcoholic,* made the *New York Times* bestseller list and was nomi-

nated for Best Political Book of the Year.

https://en.wikipedia.org/wiki/Anne_Wilson_Schaef

Another interesting source of information about Anne Wilson Schaef can be found here:

https://annewilsonschaef.com/anne-wilson-schaef/

Chapter Two

Two Types of Addicts?

First of all, I would tend to classify Addictions in TWO GROUPS – Two Types:

The MAINSTREAM Addictions.

And not only the conventional idea of Chemical Addictions but Idea- and Action-based ones too.

***

And, secondly,

The DISPLACEMENT Addiction.

Wherein someone has an Addiction to seeing – or having a hand in - some people suffering.

Furthermore, the author believes that the word, **Sociopathy** – aka Psychopathy – simply refers to the use of Displacement on a chronic basis – as an Addiction, thus.

And too, that the term "Narcissism', refers to a combination of perhaps two Main Ways in life:

The seeing of oneself – or one's Group – as Better than Others or Other Groups.

Secondly, the desire to see some people suffer – which again ties in with Sociopathy as I define it – and perhaps somewhat as Dr. Hare does, too:

Without Conscience: The Disturbing World of the Psychopaths Among Us

https://a.co/d/f8MXhL3

***

Now, here is an interesting video:

Malignant Narcissism: Psychopathy, Sociopathy, and Antisociality

https://youtu.be/B8pBbpo-CJY?si=E8vC3SR0sWOK2_Ik

Chapter Three

Do We Notice the Addictions All Around Us?

I would next bring up the interesting idea that ***many of us might not be even noticing the totality of the addictions in life.***

For consider, Sun Tzu, in The Art of War, urged us to Know ourselves and our "enemies": competitors, I'd say].

https://commons.wikimedia.org/wiki/File:Enchoen27n3200.jpg#/media/File:Enchoen27n3200.jpg

And Socrates also urged us to know ourselves:

https://www.deepthinkers.net/what-did-socrates-mean-when-he-said-know-thyself/

But ponder this:

How can we know ourselves, if we don't see many of the Defense Mechanisms – the Addictions, thus – that are so often used, and not called such?

But instead are often referred to as either Virtues, or else of No Consequence.

Noticing, too, that Robert Greene, an author, who wrote The 48 Laws of Power, for instance, has strongly urged us to evaluate people more carefully, to thus observe people much better..

Might we say, to observe their Defense Mechanisms much better – including the ones very, very commonplace and often regarded as virtues, and their non-use as seemingly pathological?

Robert Greene: The Key to Becoming a Superior Observer

https://www.youtube.com/watch?v=jI4xwd_8xbI&pp=ygUjcm9iZXJ0IGdyZWV

lbmUgYmUgYSBiZXR0ZXIgb2JzZXJ2Z
XI%3D

Additionally, at this point in the video, Mr. Greene talks of those who hire people they later are regretful for having hired, due to a lack of keen observing:

But observing of what? Perhaps, of the various Defense Mechanisms being used – the various Non-Chemical Drugs used, as per behaviors and Core Premises which are incorrect?

Chapter Four

Can Toxic Religions be An Addiction?

Indeed, when Karl Marx talked of religion being the Opium of the People, https://en.wikipedia.org/wiki/Opium_of_the_people, might he have been referring to Toxic Religions – perhaps what we might want to consider to be Cults?

In which, one might argue, one or more Core Denials – of Realtiy – are involved, are Underpinnings?

And too, that by the word "Opium", we might simply replace this term with Drug – of a Non-Chemical, idea-nature – call it a False Premise – or set of such?

Which acts like a Tranquilizer for our fears – our catastrophizings?

And thus, a set of Defense Mechanisms that acts like a Drug Cocktail?

Or a Set of Opiums, one might say? Or Anesthetics?

WE might also look at

When Religion Is an Addiction,

by Robert N. Minor:

https://whosoever.org/when-religion-is-an-a
ddiction/

Chapter Five

Denial as an Addiction Substance

Indeed, the author believes that not just Chemicals – to include alcohol, meth, fentinyl, cocaine, and so on, are drugs – chronically used defense mechanisms – but too,

the various DENIALS, too.

Or, as the person in AA says, "Stinking Thinking"?

Or the Cognitive Behavioral Therapist talks of as Dysfunctional Core Beliefs?

For consider,

The Role of Denial in Addiction

by Shahram Heshmat Ph.D.

https://www.psychologytoday.com/us/blog/science-choice/201811/the-role-denial-in-addiction

O, what some refer to as Limiting Beliefs?

Or Shinn refered to as Logjams?

Florence Scovel Shinn

See this quote by her, too, here:

“The game of life is a game of boomerangs. Our thoughts, deeds and words return to us sooner or later with astounding accuracy.”

https://www.goodreads.com/author/quotes/56422.Florence_Scovel_Shinn

Chapter Six

Alcohol - a Biological Issue, or a Coping Mechanism to Address Very Complex Problems in Living?

Personally, I would have to say, finally, that I find it very hard to wrap my head around the idea that chemical addictions are any different than an "Idea-Addiction", or an "Activity-Addiction".

For they all appear to be dodging Reality.

Just like Blame-Shifting does, or call it Rationalizing, if you will.

***

For, when the going gets tough, do many of us "Throw in the Towel", and declare that the situation is Impossible?

That it is "BROKEN"?

That WE are Broken?

Chemically?

Yet, if our computer has a software virus, we might think twice before declaring that our computer has a BROKEN BRAIN, chemically, and instead do whatever it takes to try to get to the root of the problem....

Similarly, if we were to wake up one morning and go online and see that our bank suddenly says our account balance is ZERO, would we take it at face value if told that the bank's computers have a biochemical problem – a BROKEN BRAIN – and walk away?

Yes, the problems we have, in life – including getting to the moon, in the 1960s, can be utterly complex. But is complexity reason enough to say that the SITUATION is BROKEN?

Thus urging someone to TOSS the PROBLEM – the ADDICTION, in this case – in the DEMSEY DUMPSTER – as a HUMPTY DUMPTY Problem, because unsolvable presently, by All the King's Men and All the King's Horses?

Or do we have a glimmer or more of hope, as Marie Forleo mentions, in her book, "Everything is Figureoutable"?

(To a large degree?)

Everything Is Figureoutable Paperback

https://a.co/d/jdWihU7

***

In this vein, I would like to mention a good video – that talks of how a man and later, a tribe, of Native American Indians, made great headway on the Chemical Addiction known as Alcoholism:

The Honour of All: the Story of Alkali Lake

A website makes some commentary on it, at,

https://ammsa.com/publications/windspeaker/alkali-lake-shows-way

Chapter Seven

A Brief Video for Uplifting Information on Ourselves?

Dr. Alain de Botton, a Swiss-born philosopher and psychologist, now living in England, has a most interesting and helpful video here:

Alain de Botton | A Therapeutic Journey - Lessons from the School of Life

https://youtu.be/mRJ7TeJEMao?si=1kj8n5do4YqlEgwn

Chapter Eight

The Beginning of My Growth in Addiction Knowledge..

This author applies a massive amount of skill in mathematics, and fifteen years' use of a software program known as SuperMemo, to this topic of addictions.

***

Next, the author seeks to apply only deterministic words, including, when it comes to people, in this case. Which means having the utmost of Respect for all others and himself too.

The author created two hundred of these, at a minimum, over five years.

Because the words had to be invented, not plucked off a shelf.

Many of the ideas in this short book – or outline of a topic, to be more exact – are not likely to be found in academic books – in other words, books created by those who have graduated from a college.

Or who have majored in psychology, or have degrees and certifications in addictions.

Because the very subject matter tends to be "data-smogged", the author believes, in an academic approach.

***

Instead, the author has approached the topic by observation, time visiting people in facilities as part of such, and a general non-academic approach, as mentioned by Henry David Thoreau

"I went to the woods because I wished to live deliberately, to front only the essential facts of life, and see if I could not learn what it had to teach, and not, when I came to die, discover that I had not lived. I did not wish to live what was not life, living is so dear; nor did I wish to practice resignation, unless it was quite necessary. I wanted to live deep and suck out all the marrow of life, to live so sturdily and Spartan-like as to put to rout all that was not life, to cut a broad swath and shave close, to drive life into a corner, and reduce it to its lowest terms, and, if it proved to be mean, why then to get the whole and genuine meanness of it, and publish its meanness to the world; or if it were sublime, to know it by experience, and be able to give a true account of it in my next excursion."

Henry David Thoreau

***

The author, too, has enjoyed nature greatly:

Author at age of about one

Indeed, the author had a year-long break from school, after Kindergarten, and spent almost all of that time playing in the woods of North Carolina, including collecting box turtles, insects, leaves, and watching birds.

When he was a youth, he alternated living in Minnesota, during the school year, and his grandparents' farm in Michigan.

My mother skiing outside our home in Minnesota.

The author's summer time – farm and more...

Author, mother, and sister on his grandparents' Michigan farm, age five.

Author, seven, left; mother, right; great-grandmother, behind us.

Lake where the author boated daily, on the farm, during summers, age seven to fifteen:

Mother, sister, and author, on Michigan farm

And when he spent three years in Southern California, he hiked on weekends with the Sierra Club.

And when he was 37, he packed two duffle bags and boarded a Greyhound bus and went to a village of eight hundred people, near the Mississippi River, and also near the Illinois/Iowa border, to contemplate life more fully – doing without a car there – and taking only one book with him – Walden, again, by Henry David Thoreau.

To my parents, who made this possible.

For instance, my mother, an immigrant from eastern Poland, having come to America at the age of twelve, after a two-week long boat journey, to Ellis Island....

My mother as a young gal in Europe,
before coming to America

And to my father, too, a most astute Trainer in life....

Brought up in the ghettos of Philadelphia; left school at the age of seventeen; and later acquired a GED and went on to obtain a Ph.D . degree at a major University in English Literature; this led to my interest and pursuit of writing at a very early age; and too, concerning his love of photography, both of these areas, rubbing off on me: hence, "The apple doesn't fall far from the tree"?

Training!

Then, too, my grandparents:
For significantly, my grandmother raised me
during my first four years, in my waking hours.
And her husband – my grandfather – worked in
the tool and die industry for cars; she was born
in eastern Poland, like my mother, and was a
farmer there; he was born in Odesa, Ukraine,
and a Mennonite, and herb collector and maker
of many grandfather clocks in his spare time, on
their farm in Michigan:

Grandparents in Niagara Falls, I believe

And to my farm experience, as a youth, each summer, in Michigan:

Then, too, to a man of the greatest impact upon myself, too, from the ages of twelve to fourteen, starting when I first sought him out to help me obtain a ham radio license at the age of twelve:

Mr. Foster; who interestingly did have a foster child he raised when I knew him; he helped me obtain my ham license; he hunted; he took me to ham conventions and camped with me; he collected stamps and coins; and let me build electronic projects in his workshop; and even took me for a ride on his motorcycle, popping a wheelie

And finally, to "Religion":

Again, that of my grandmother, a Baptist; and my grandfather, a Mennonite from Ukraine - born in the city of Odessa.

The ethnic Baptist church I attended in the summers, when a youth, while on the farm the other six days of the week... German was spoken.

...

And to my parents' religious influence upon myself, too: for they almost became missionar-

ies in the Plymouth Brethren Church – a group similar to the Amish, Mennonites, and Quakers: they were to be posted to Canada.
And to L'abri, started by Francis Schaeffer.
Whereupon I spent a week in training at the Massachusetts branch, in 1982.

And later, other faiths, too....
Including the faith of the Native American Indians, whom I first came into contact with when living in California, having spent time exploring Arizona, and too, in Cherokee, North Carolina, and Vonure, Tennessee:

I made a visit to Vonure, Tennessee, in 2021, to learn more about the Cherokee Indians. Amongst the sights was the Sequoya Birthplace Museum, featuring Sequoya, who had single-handedly created the Cherokee alphabet, under great duress. I again camped, this time in the Cherokee National Park near Vonure, for several days

REFUND INFORMATION

REFUND INFORMATION

Desire a refund? No problem: 100% refund, for any reason at all, and absolutely no questions asked, period. And no time limit on this offer. I recognize that sometimes, purchased items are discovered to simply not be a "good fit", or for any number of other reasons....

Loran Joly

If for any reason you desire a refund or desire to leave a comment,

please contact me at:

message@goldpogo.com

or

ReEnvision Press
Box #1036
1303 US 127 South
Suite 104
Frankfort, KY 40601

www.ingramcontent.com/pod-product-compliance
Lightning Source LLC
Chambersburg PA
CBHW041652150726
48005CB00013BA/1676

* 9 7 9 8 8 6 9 1 3 1 7 4 4 *